Plans Deranged by Time
The Poetry of George Fetherling

Plans Deranged by Time
The Poetry of George Fetherling

Selected
with an
introduction by
A.F. Moritz

**WILFRID LAURIER
UNIVERSITY PRESS**

Wilfrid Laurier University Press acknowledges the support of the Canada Council for the Arts for its publishing program. We acknowledge the financial support of the Government of Canada through the Canada Book Fund for our publishing activities.

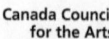 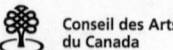 

Library and Archives Canada Cataloguing in Publication

Fetherling, George, [date]
  [Poems. Selections]
    Plans deranged by time : the poetry of George Fetherling / selected with an introduction by A.F. Moritz and an afterword by George Fetherling.

(Laurier poetry series)
Includes bibliographical references.
Issued also in electronic formats.
ISBN 978-1-55458-631-8

  I. Moritz, A. F.   II. Title.   III. Series: Laurier poetry series

PS8561.E834A6 2012   C811'.54   C2011-908429-5

Electronic monograph.
Issued also in print format.
ISBN 978-1-55458-648-6 (PDF).—ISBN 978-1-55458-649-3 (EPUB)

  I. Moritz, A. F.   II. Title.   III. Series: Laurier poetry series (Online)

PS8561.E834A6 2012   C811'.54   C2011-908430-9

© 2012 Wilfrid Laurier University Press
Waterloo, Ontario N2L 3C5, Canada
www.wlupress.wlu.ca

Cover photograph by Joe Lepiano. Cover design and text design by P.J. Woodland.

This book is printed on FSC recycled paper and is certified Ecologo. It is made from 100% post-consumer fibre, processed chlorine free, and manufactured using biogas energy.

Every reasonable effort has been made to acquire permission for copyright material used in this text, and to acknowledge all such indebtedness accurately. Any errors and omissions called to the publisher's attention will be corrected in future printings.

No part of this publication may be reproduced, stored in a retrieval system or transmitted, in any form or by any means, without the prior written consent of the publisher or a licence from The Canadian Copyright Licensing Agency (Access Copyright). For an Access Copyright licence, visit www.accesscopyright.ca or call toll free to 1-800-893-5777.

Table of Contents

Foreword, *Neil Besner* / vii
Biographical Note / viii
Introduction, *A.F. Moritz* / ix

Alleycat / 1
Harry's New York Bar in Paris / 2
Border Catechism *(excerpts)* / 3
Subroutine / 4
The Dark Grid / 5
The Six O'Clock News from Buffalo / 6
Moving towards the Vertical Horizon *(excerpts)* / 8
Memorandum for the File / 12
Pre Texts / 13
Radio / 14
Ancient Beliefs / 16
Telegraphic Instructions / 18
Beginning with North / 19
The View Keeps Reminding Us of Flags / 20
With the Name Goes Great Responsibility / 21
Opportunities for Redemption / 23
Chinese Anthology *(excerpts)* / 24
Mother Goddess / 26
Art Criticism / 27
Juice / 29
Ice Ages / 30
Old Chinese Poem / 31

Bush Architecture / 32
0930 / 33
Letter Two *(excerpt)* / 34
Singer, An Elegy *(excerpts)* / 35
First Signs of Wartime Spring / 50
Navigating Chinatown / 52
Confusion of Themes Not of Motives / 53
Mappamundi / 54
Postdated / 56
Afterword, *George Fetherling* / 57
Acknowledgements / 60

Foreword

Early in the twenty-first century, poetry in Canada—writing and publishing it, reading and thinking about it—finds itself in a strangely conflicted place. We have many strong poets continuing to produce exciting new work, and there is still a small audience for poetry; but increasingly, poetry is becoming a vulnerable art, for reasons that don't need to be rehearsed.

But there are things to be done: we need more real engagement with our poets. There needs to be more access to their work in more venues—in classrooms, in the public arena, in the media—and there need to be more, and more different kinds, of publications that make the wide range of our contemporary poetry more widely available.

The hope that animates this series from Wilfrid Laurier University Press is that these volumes help to create and sustain the larger readership that contemporary Canadian poetry so richly deserves. Like our fiction writers, our poets are much celebrated abroad; they should just as properly be better known at home.

Our idea is to ask a critic (sometimes himself a poet) to select thirty-five poems from across a poet's career; write an engaging, accessible introduction; and have the poet himself—in this case, George Fetherling—write an afterword. In this way, we think that the usual practice of teaching a poet through eight or twelve poems from an anthology is much improved upon; and readers in and out of classrooms will have more useful, engaging, and comprehensive introductions to a poet's work. Readers might also come to see more readily, we hope, the connections among, as well as the distances between, the life and the work.

It was the ending of an Al Purdy poem that gave Margaret Laurence the epigraph for *The Diviners*: "but they had their being once / and left a place to stand on." Our poets still do, and they are leaving many places to stand on. We hope that this series helps, variously, to show how and why this is so.

—*Neil Besner*
General Editor

Biographical Note

George Fetherling, a wide-ranging and prolific figure in Canadian literature, was born in 1949 and has lived and worked as a writer in London, New York, and, for the past forty-five years, Toronto, the city with which he is most closely identified. He began publishing poetry in the mid-1960s and works in both the long-form mode, as in *Singer, An Elegy* (2004), and in the lyrical, as in *The Sylvia Hotel Poems* (2010). He also has written four book-length fictions, the best known of which is the novel *Walt Whitman's Secret* (2010).

He has been intimately involved with cultural commentary, independent-press publishing, book culture, and book history. He has often been called a man of letters ("an accusation I take pleasure in denying") simply because he has published in so many different genres. These range from works on Canadian history (for example, *The Gold Crusades: A Social History of Gold Rushes,* 1997) to travel narratives such as *Three Pagodas Pass: A Roundabout Journey to Burma* (2004) and *Indochina Now and Then* (2012). Among his dozens of other books is a biography, *The Gentle Anarchist: A Life of George Woodcock*, which appeared in 1998, three years after its subject's death.

Fetherling's most popular prose work remains *Travels by Night: A Memoir of the Sixties*. First published in 1994, it concerns his contemporaries in the great Canadian cultural renaissance of the 1960s and 1970s and his own heavily textured background ("I have no lifestyle, only a *modus operandi*"). Fetherling is also a visual artist.

He has received the Harbourfront Festival Prize "for a substantial contribution to Canadian letters" and a D. Litt. *honoris causa* from St. Mary's University for "an instrumental role in the development" of Canadian writing. He has been writer-in-residence at Queen's University, the University of New Brunswick, and the University of Toronto. He is widely anthologized. The Montreal *Gazette* has called him "a mercurial, liberal intelligence [...] the kind of which English Canada has too short a supply." *Xtra* described him as "something of a national literary treasure."

Introduction

One of the archetypal characters of the modern imagination is the impeccable but threadbare man glimpsed moving through the crowds, scarcely a shadow, or walking along a wall, nearly merging with the twilight: a mysterious character who, if encountered, reveals a combination of the aristocratic mind, the man of honour, and the poet. This is the figure that the verse of George Fetherling raises in our hearts, which then are made to become the cityscape he crosses and goes to ground in, in which he's almost an alien and an outcast but which strangely he possesses more fully than do the solid citizen, the politician, the technocrat, the business person. The alleys, the poor rented rooms, the minuscule dramas or expanses of *noia* passing under weak, acidic light in abandoned precincts, move forward and take their rightful place as facets of the city equal to any others. Better than equal: the repositories of the reality that belongs solely to poverty and struggle, and that has been removed from the artificial world of technique, publicity and wealth. Hence, these lost zones display their symbolic character as images of the truth of many an experience that would seem to be their opposite, occurring in the busy plazas and shopping districts and splendid towers and clubs, in the midst of crowds intent to enact in some cases a businesslike, in others a manic, satisfaction: a truth that irrupts only when suffering and isolation penetrate this bright facade, as inevitably, for everyone, they must.

This haunting and haunted character permeates *Plans Deranged by Time: The Poetry of George Fetherling*, and in this the poems selected reflect the temper of his eleven volumes of verse, from *Our Man in Utopia* (Macmillan, 1971) to *The Sylvia Hotel Poems* (Quattro, 2010). In the first poem here, the singing voice identifies with an alley cat, and lyric imagination follows the small beast, returned by night to freedom, wildness, and vulnerability. Its nocturnal patrol of images has something to do with the poet's human experience, something to do with his observation of urban cats, and something to do with the generous library of fictional and filmic precedents he carries inside him:

> Simultaneous with this writing
> the dull salutes of keys on paper
> I live again
>   like an alleycat
> silent on bricks and concrete
> nimble on ledges and fire escapes

> Back of the Yards
>   crossing the street
> only when necessary
> and then very quickly . . .

And in the second-last poem chosen, "Mappamundi," the poet wants to summon "all the travellers / passing through" to have them experience their ultimate distance from the smallest, most essential versions of an integrated society, couples who reply "to either's silence with the silence of the two together." In this poem we glimpse the human environment of the isolated speaker as he registers his separation from the loved one. She is a specific woman, but in the context of the book she converges with humanity, as represented in its most cherished productions, especially the modern city, its home. In this home, the singing voice has a poor room, so it somehow has a place there yet it is far separated too:

> Cracks in the ceiling plaster are the rivers
> of your body. In the patterns of the mutilated lino
> I find faces, yours and those of saints and
> everybody's favourite sacred parent.

Fetherling has always had his own characteristic understanding and version of this modern archetype, which emerges as early as the original picaresque, *Lazarillo de Tormes* (in the person of Lazarillo's second master, the impoverished knight), is fully realized by Poe (in the narrator / subject doppelganger of "The Man of the Crowd" and in Poe himself), and thence passed on to Dickens, Melville, Baudelaire, Dostoevsky, Hamsun, Kafka, and many others. We thus can find Fetherling related to the early Eliot, but he has found ways to escape Eliot's domination, both in the texture of his verse and more particularly in his dramatic approach.

    The first lines of "Alleycat" identify the poet's feline wanderings as a simile for his shaping and vivifying his experience in the creation of poetry: "Simultaneous with this writing / the dull salutes of keys on paper / I live again . . ." The separation of the third line into two halves, "I live again / like an alleycat" allows the poem to start with a grand upthrust of assertive energy in three words before it falls to rehearsing the poor appearances of this life

> seen for an instant under some arc lamp
> in the flashlight of some cop
> or the headlight of a lonely car
> no one knowing
>   whether it was me

or a crumpled piece of sports page
carried on a burst of wind
that seemed to come from nowhere

Just as at the beginning of the poem the eruption of assertive creativity darts yet descends into the cat's meagre and by-its-wits existence, so at the end it rises again out of the ghost that might be only an old scrap of paper into an instance of the wind that bloweth where it listeth. The source and destination of this breath is beyond human ken: "nowhere" catches up the contemptuous sense of the word, you're a nobody from nowhere, and merges it with a transcendence, the nowhere and nothing that is the only true fullness and wealth. Kenosis. Poverty. Freedom. But it's a freedom asserted against the strangely simultaneous reality of the restriction of exclusion, the person who, alone, must contemplate the patterns of ceiling cracks and the scoring in cheap linoleum floors, and find there something to cherish and to remind him of the loved one and the great world. The person who constantly struggles against self-contempt and despair because of his hard-up, disregarded state.

The poems show Fetherling as a true poet: an artist who feels, sees and thinks through images, their indefinable linkages, and the music and tone that accompanies the verbal image and carries it into the heart. His multiform career threatens to distract us from this. He has written novels, essays, travel books, biographies, film and art criticism, and nonfiction works on a wide assortment of subjects (such as assassinations!), and has been constantly occupied as a reviewer and commentator, frequently as a publisher and newspaper journalist. He is, it might seem, a *gendelettres* (person of letters) and an intellectual who simply includes in the panoply of his work a certain amount of poetry. And in some ways, his verse itself might seem to confirm this. It has formal resemblances to that of some of the scholar-poets (though Fetherling is an autodidact and a reader, not a university-trained scholar) and author-poets of the mid-twentieth century: Robert Fitzgerald, Horace Gregory, Dudley Fitts, Lawrence Durrell, or the fine translations that have been made of Julio Cortázar's and Günter Grass's poetry. Probably this is not a matter of influence but of the fact that, like the other North American poets maturing in the 1950s and 1960s, Fetherling worked in the aftermath of Pound and Eliot. Like the American poets named above (as opposed to, say, the "Beat" group and the Black Mountain group, though like them embracing the help of William Carlos Williams and his followers and Kenneth Rexroth), he tried to deflect those influences into something that recaptured elements of classic English poetry while fully retaining modernity, its speed, vividness, and liberty of subject, rhythm and expression. There was a desire among such poets to put the dynamic precision that Pound developed most brilliantly in the flow of *The Cantos* into shapely lyrics which suggested, rather than spread, beyond their boundaries.

More particularly, though, his originality lies in absorbing his aspirations as *gendelettres* and public intellectual into his poetry, and creating a composite figure whose feelings and thoughts have behind them the melancholy weight of the exile of intellectualism and literary cultivation within North America. For the North American person of letters and intellectual live the "marginal" life I mentioned above. Most previous examples of the symbolic figure we've examined have taken the form of a representative person who possesses cultural attainments, yes, but whose essential characteristic is that of being a poet, whether specifically or not. As poet, he or she vividly, paradigmatically lives the placelessness of the sensitive and aspiring person in a world of despised ideals, omnipresent technical pride and power, banal pragmatism, and an unthematized, automatic atheism that makes spare time and distractions the only remaining echoes of spirit and freedom. Walter Martin well characterizes this figure in reference to Baudelaire: "A poet's freedom ... is the freedom of one who knows he will never be anything but a failure in the world's estimation, and may do as he pleases" (*Charles Baudelaire: Complete Poems*, trans. Walter Martin, 2002, p. 438).

To this figure, Fetherling adds the intellectual and the person of letters. Yvon Grenier defines a *gendelettres* as a "highly cultivated but contemplative individual whose influence on public affairs is either nil or unintentional," as compared with the intellectual, who "may typically be defined as someone who is recognized by society's cultural participants as well read and cultivated, and who successfully uses this cultural capital to justify ... public interventions on social issues." Grenier observes that "[i]ntellectuals are a product of modernity, but modernization and democratization usually bring about the decline of the role of intellectual and the ascent of the professional," while the "*gendelettres* has always had and is likely to retain a fairly marginal role." In a comment reminiscent of the narrow neglected margins, the neighbourhoods down back of the stockyards, in Fetherling's poetry, he continues, "Nowadays, would-be intellectuals have no political *space* [my emphasis]: politicians and lobbyists monopolize access to political power. The media play the role of intermediary between the political class and the apathetic masses. In cities, a new knowledge class of lifestyle engineers or moral entrepreneurs strives to shape specific social activities or 'issues' (the environment, gender, taxes, and so on)" (Yvon Grenier, *From Art to Politics: Octavio Paz and the Pursuit of Freedom*, 2001, pp. 17–18).

In "The Dark Grid" Fetherling refers to a life in "the cracks" and this appeals to me as a better metaphor than the current-to-the-point-of-cliché "margins." In the seams of the almost seamless world of power, wealth and publicity, the alley cat and the poet-intellectual find narrow spaces in which, nevertheless, to flourish: the seamy side, or sides, of contemporary life, a polyseamy of rooms and narrow passages both of the city and the spirit. Fetherling's exile figure, an urban rat, passing almost unseen among us, carries through the bustling, glinting streets of crowds and glass a secret cargo of broad knowledge and the perspective it brings, a gift that desires to be given and has to ask itself constantly whether it is a gift at all, since no one wants it, or even perceives it. Fetherling's figure lives this quandary doubly, in that as a non-scholar but a true intellectual he does not have even the enclave of the university. By the same token, he has no temptation to live within any intellectual ghetto as a world, to advance its pride against the pride of other sectors, to overestimate the importance it does possess, to undermine its real claims by an immaturely imbalanced proclamation that turns them to overstatement. On the contrary, if there is exaggeration in Fetherling's speaker, it's a litotes of humility and invisibility sometimes bordering on humiliation. Belittlement.

The sense of unheeded isolation is sometimes projected into observations and characters, sometimes directly espoused by the speaker. In "Harry's New York Bar in Paris," at the beginning of the selection, there are the customers who

> mumble
> amen into their drinks
> to combat power withdrawal

The very title of "Subroutine" as a label for the speaker's life is significant, and the poem avers that

> One grows resigned
> to living in a house where
> pictures always need
> straightening
> and sleep comes on hot
> nights thus . . .
>
> There are bottles
> being smashed and Jamaican
> imprecations and another
> sound that could be weeping
> or then again might be laughter

The cracks, interstices, brief seconds of salvation that are the whole of life for the marginal character, the character of the seams, are seen twofold in "Opportunities for Redemption"—firstly as the "nick of time" of some obscure escape the speaker has achieved, and secondly as the lonesome evening, abed before sleep and thinking back:

> Deliverance in the nick of time
> is the highlight of my day,
> the part I look forward to
> and reflect on at night
> during someone else's watch;
> I imagine you are the same.

Sometimes the character pauses to examine himself in the rituals and the work of sustaining this unnoticed life, for instance in "Letter Two":

> I would go to thrift shops searching for the rejected books,
> the most obsolete clothes, thoroughly discarded decorative objects.
> I made a little museum on the walls of my bedroom. There were old
> newspapers, photographs on stiff card of unidentified persons
> thrown out when other persons died . . .

This passage comes from a poem about the speaker's grasp that history is useless and in the vastness and relentlessness of modernity has (at least as formerly conceived) disappeared altogether. But the lines leap out at us as a perfect description of the daily doings of Fetherling's characteristic poetic speaker, reflectively intensified in a sort of self-commiseration, a developed taste for the desolate, a sucking of the sore tooth of banishment and solitude, that is made into emotion, not sentimentality, by its precision and compassion.

Neither the frustrated aspiration to social and political effectiveness that belongs to the intellectual, nor the *gendelettres'* awareness of his more-than-ever exiguous status in contemporary society, issues in political poems. Both by poetic parentage and by emotional disposition, Fetherling belongs to the Audenesque, disabused, "poetry makes nothing happen" strain of thinking. Social ideals and ideas are present as implications, usually regrets. There are outbursts of a fervour of revolt:

> I can't stand the silence.
> My ears chafe waiting
> for the tune of a catchy explosion.
> I am the neighbourhood dynamiter
> who never knows when opportunity

> might strike. One must always
> be alert and heavily armed
> against success and its enemies.
>
> ("Art Criticism")

But despite this occasional note (which itself ends in the idea of self-destruction: "I will be scattered over a wide area. / Parts of me may never be found"), there is none even of Auden's vigorousness of detailed commentary from the sidelines; criticism takes the form of melancholy awareness of being swept along in a heedless flood, and what the intellectual knows and could offer is left implicit, a matter of the tone of suppression:

> The Americans have a new war
> that's how we know the generations have changed
> but we're not headlines . . .
>
> The strategy is to let the future emerge
> a little at a time that we might grow accustomed
> and not protest or go mad.
> The window opens so briefly that we cannot
> throw out the words.
> This will have to do for now.

Later in the same poem ("First Signs of Wartime Spring"), the speaker offers the advice, "Be like the cave-dwelling hermit / who learns from the mute / and mocks the big yellow bruise": here is another image of finding a not-yet-overrun hole in which one can still live.

Lying in such a hole, the speaker of "Opportunities for Redemption," quoted above, says, "I imagine you are much the same." The other side of Fetherling's mapping of suppression by and within the society which claims one as a participant is an intense sympathy for all others who are similarly caught and simultaneously cast out. It is a sympathy for the part in everyone that endures this dilemma, which is one of the chief ones of modernity. Through it, Fetherling's relentlessly personal and lyric poetry is unmistakably political and social.

The note of exhortation in the form of wisdom-statement ("Be like the cave-dwelling hermit . . .") reappears frequently, most often in an intimate register that bespeaks the lyric self's desire to have something to show for his experience, and something to offer to at least one other. Equally frequent is the concentration upon characters, such as the despondent drinkers in Harry's New York Bar, mentioned earlier, or the educative vision of "an old woman in a straw hat / who leads her buffalo home from the fields" at the end of "Juice." But it is in Fetherling's finest work, *Singer, An Elegy* (2004), that the various strands of self-examination and implicit social vision come together under the sign of sympathy. Here the urge to fellow-feeling arising from the speaker's imaginative grasp of his own situation melds into paradoxical intimacy with an unknowable other. This leads to examination of the speaker's own provenance, and rich social and historical commentary detailing the nearly intangible influences of times and societies on character.

It's a poem that sings and thinks richly of the ancient quandary of fate, chance and freedom: which is real, and if all are real, how do they mix? Chance inhabits it from the very title, the fact that the poet's father was named "Singer." This fact also invites us to associate the lyric speaker more than usually closely with the author of the book. The speaker is a mask perhaps only in the sense that we observe the author groping to form a face, an attitude, which constantly changes. In keeping with this, the form of the poem participates in the blurring of genres which is a chief modern genre itself: the free form sequential poem is also a memoir, the biography is also a vehicle of social and religious speculation and of self-examination on the part of the biographer. Philosophically, the scrutiny of the contemporary sense of the self's isolation within itself, and of the ultimate unknowability ("alterity") of another, becomes a constant loving return to the other, an accompanying of the dead. Chance, which may also take the form of an underserved gift, lies in the details the speaker happens to possess of Singer, and the memories among so many lost that deign to surface and bring back again a certain presence: favourite phrases of the dead man, an inventory of his tools, his predilections and habits. The excellence of the poem is in the interplay of these things, which well represents the webwork of a life, and the way the mind, when most aware through memory and thought of its aloneness, is most together with the past, the people, and the surrounding society that are its substance. In this richness, bewilderment is veined by a sorrowful communion-in-isolation that seems now a prophecy of true community, now the poignant likelihood that this poor reality of gratitude in the midst of loss and isolation is the best we will ever have:

> I failed, it flows back over me like a welcoming tide.
> Who knew it could be this warm?
>
> I feel completed by not being whole ...

That, but also this:

> A prayer to the river gods might commence:
>
> Please I can't die yet, there's
> so much healing to do.
>
> That would be mine. Would it also
> be his? I don't know how
>
> we struggle on as we do . . .

—A.F. Moritz

Alleycat

Simultaneous with this writing
the dull salutes of keys on paper
I live again
           like an alleycat
silent on bricks and concrete
nimble on ledges and fire escapes
Back of the Yards
                crossing the street
only when necessary
and then very quickly
                  head and tail
downward
        the shortest path
between two points indistinct
in the night
           then disappearing
into the shadows on the other side
seen for an instant under some arc lamp
in the flashlight of some cop
or the headlight of a lonely car
no one knowing
                whether it was me
or a crumpled piece of sports page
carried on a burst of wind
that seemed to come from nowhere

Harry's New York Bar in Paris

The bored waiter moves
towards you like a shark
in an aquarium
                  turning quickly
when very close
having lived here many years
he knows the limits
and where the glass is
and is able to seem
calmly efficient
                  while ignoring
the customers the dramaturges
who anoint themselves
                  and mumble
amen into their drinks
to combat power withdrawal

What you think is the mood
is really the smell
                  the threat
of posterity that keeps them
on their toes
            all the colours
have to be imported
nightly smoke is flown in
                    special
like the noise
of the telephone ringing
with calls from persons long dead
and Cole Porter's ghost
                  playing
the piano

Border Catechism *(excerpts)*

What is the nature of your visit?

To observe the passing seasons
on the ground and to study
geometry from above . . .

I want to see the city close up and how
it runs together in a kind of neon autumn
quiet optimism wrenched from bankruptcy sales
the miles of donut shops with karate schools upstairs
cinemas becoming bingo halls
when the people inside them
find their concentration waning

And yet I want to glide above it
for one never knows a city till one
learns it from the air
and sees how small it is and who
supports it with their lives
and what a struggle it is to linger
just a while longer in the clearing
when the forest is so near and the
aeroplanes overhead

Subroutine

One grows resigned
to living in a house where
pictures always need
straightening
and sleep comes on hot
nights thus:

a burial at sea;
the board is tilted and
one slips silently
below the surface where
noises though muted
stand out all the more

There are bottles
being smashed and Jamaican
imprecations and another
sound that could be weeping
but then again might be laughter

and most especially the CPR heading eastward
as trains almost never do,
shaking bits of plaster
from the ceiling
raising puffs of dust
on the floor

Some night when we
have been properly conditioned
the bed may shake
though no train passes by
and telephone rings become
emphatic

until the morning when
we wake up
dead inside our clothes

The Dark Grid

In the cracks of this white city
there is another grid
                where applause
and politics do not exist
and politeness doesn't matter
You have seen me there
and know I only know the back doors
of restaurants
their distinctive arrays of garbage
little brick holes that are warm
for those not confused by purpose
a few spent aspirations perhaps
but no purely theoretical contempt

Personally I no longer care
whether sleep is deserved or broken
by men at grimy loading docks
hurrying off into sunlight
                      No one
works for the government here
however indirectly
                no one has received
any mail in years
though you may write me if you wish
in care of the pigeons

The Six O'Clock News from Buffalo

Once there
were streamers to greet
each famous visitor

these turned
to cobwebs
before they disappeared

and waterfalls
became escalators
which finally broke down

in the sure-footed
progress of decay

with its gaudy colours
pinball lighting
and not unpleasant odour

that's carried across
the lake
with a faint suggestion
of all-time polka hits

Where are
the Natives of Cheektowaga
Tonawanda Lackawanna
gone these two hundred years
nearly as extinct as the
foundry worker
the housewife in Depew
we're told of breathlessly
with mock grimness
as the music swells

Why is the politician outside
the courthouse hiding
behind his hat

who knocked over the
elemental liquor store

who set the fire
on Genesee Street
that burns oblivious

like
some eternal flame

Moving towards the Vertical Horizon *(excerpts)*

i.

Once it's written down it's no longer true

When you create a file you are dealing
with stillborn information

Photographs have been worthless
since it became so easy to enhance them

When there is no means of giving proof
there is no reason for anyone to hide

Everybody stays silent

Not exactly what St Anthony had in mind

ii.

Christ was alive
one of only 300 million
when Natives met here
to trade and discarded
these broken tools
in what, then as now,
was alluvial mud

(each spring the stream
runs high and cold)

they didn't know of Him
nor He of them;

at Contact, say 1600, there were only 500 million
persons on the earth,
by 1750 still only 700 million
the aboriginals already proscribed
doomed;

by 2010 you will have your choice
of 35 cities with over 8 million
people apiece

the rich with concertina wire
and broken glass atop floodlit
garden walls,
the others in corrugated tin shacks
if they're lucky
if they're not among those
taken out by disease;

cities maybe but not metropolitan
for there is no polis
but a new distinction not yet
coined, only to be lost—
some other generation can
recover it

Look at your density map and see
where there are fewest, and go there

take up what was dropped as worthless

prove to these skeletons they were wrong

iii.

If you don't have possessions
then you don't have to break as they do

though you still make choices
this is one of the rules so easy
to remember

do you pick an eminence
that defends itself and rely
on cisterns
or remain in the valley
water's flowing there
but high ground on two sides?

Flight is no escape from compromise
but a journey to find the primitives
they had good reasons for
believing as they did

Build small and build thick
several locations
a day's patrol between them
better than one big one
surrounded and surprised

There's still much to be said
for the square two-storey box
without doors or windows below
just a ladder someone lets down
or you pull up behind you
there's life in old ideas yet

The separate kitchen reduces danger
build it plumb and secure it
find the old dump now buried
for bottles broken ones

can be cut down later with ice
from the lake and fire from the sky
but use little that was made by man
no plastics, rubber, aluminium

Your best protection once
was anonymity; that didn't work
now the plan must be to go
rearrange what nature gives you

a field strewn with rock is a wall
that awaits assembly
not like the city where all was
allegory, sex a metaphor
respiration syntax

Everything was a symbol then
now everything's a kit

Memorandum for the File

i.

The sky all stained again

where the narrative leaves a trail
active but reactive also
and a shared chronology

for this is reputedly
the offspring of
another such day long ago

when morning was finally revealed
once silence reached a
crisis then broke like a fever.

ii.

Waking up, moving out
from within, an attempt
at gesture

the anonymity that
lies behind the name
and discourses most sincerely
on its meaning.

In reviewing the life we review
the method.

In souvenir of the occasion
we set down these lines.

Pre Texts

i.

Whatever we notice becomes
the landscape that documents itself

random cows graze beneath hydro pylons

white squares stiff on somebody's clothesline
except in propaganda a sight that's been obsolete for years

people in their living rooms living

a lone oak on a hilltop like a logo
a willow like an afghan hound

the Canada of the TV station sign-off
when ocean and anthem swell in agreement.

ii.

Anthropologists invaded once
the explorers' dirty work was done

same process, different perplexities

our best course now is confronting recollection
learning how circumstance favours the
higher elevations, how disputes are resolved
by the nature of things.

iii.

Irritating rain
like scratches on a classic film

ends, and a loon in the swamp bestirs itself
to recross the old denim sky.

Radio

They enter by one earphone and
leave by the other: ghost narrations.
The sound of rats or someone trying the doorknob
(I don't mean the cop on the beat)
static like the table-talk of parrots
or scarlet monkeys screeching in trees
until a voice, maybe human, speaks
but hesitates, caught for an instant
before being sucked into the blackness
like a book thrown from the window
of a train (the pages beat as quickly
as the wings of a bird that senses
some danger unheard on radio
then dies).

This is what we use now in lieu of maps.
What comes to us is where we go.
Much depends on conditions.
Jailer, I insist on an omen to subdue
my doubts or, failing that, a radio.

I hear too many nasal accents,
see too many vacancies and embalmed businesses
and railyards where the only sound of life
is freight trains having rusty sex, yawning
and stretching in the distance, running
headlong at each other like whales
(they covet our stability, we envy
them their freedom).

Up all night with the fear of death
and the radio, listening in the dark
with middle-aged wonder

reminded of the old unbearable melancholy
made worse when there was nobody
to share it (or confide it to).

My dead friends
why can't I find you on the radio?

Ancient Beliefs

Here we do
not worship ancestors
we treat them

for what they are,
part memory, part
parasitic affliction.

As one cannot prevent
them, neither can one
be completely cured
of other personalities
that persist inside our own.

Specifically,
we believe each of us
to be a pool
into which two streams empty
acid and alkaline
father and mother;
it doesn't matter which
is which, only
that there be two

recombinant, variform
fainter as we grow fainter
on the one hand Simulacrum
Recrudescence on
the other—
impressions of people
who bequeathed us all
the unused portions
of themselves.

It is also our belief
that what's not paradox
is allegory.

Telegraphic Instructions

For art's sake look out
stop regard the threat
of rain that hangs
in a discoloured sky
observe how blood
adds flavour
to the pavement
how the gutters
fill with rubbish
how old sensations
still obtain.

Stop and take under advisement
this entire sad heritage of dreams

find some interior
means of becoming
the instrument we seek.

Wake up praying and
recall the limbs of trees
motioning through the glass
once silence became obsessive;

a hole opened up in
the darkness on this
very spot

remember?

Beginning with North

First comes a white frame
house, ancient and decrepit
dignity wearing thin but upright
amid treed hills and stooped shoulders
built by someone with the grit
of summer on the back of his neck
more comfortable designing barns perhaps
but all sorts of chores in a lifetime
rough stone foundation, strong
erect skeleton and plain façade
an arrangement of perpendiculars
on a curved background, white
slats against green foliage
overhanging the dirty river;
it's the custom to paint only
one side each year
beginning with north, the hardest
a small job never finished
always a contest between owner and nature
to see who gives up first.

near Fredericton

The View Keeps Reminding Us of Flags

The view keeps reminding us of flags
we don't wish to be reminded of
certainly not now, certainly not these.

Red in the morning, sailors take warning
but do they listen? Never.

Looking northward they sense freedom
where the rest of us can only prophesy.

Boats nervous at their moorings
the wind kicks up, the last ferry
waddles across the harbour.
The lights that struggle to stay visible
grow weaker all the same.
It's like something out of Bullfinch.
This ferry only goes one way!
And where exactly does that leave
the living? Exactly.

The eye of the storm, the eye
of the beholder of the storm: streaks
unfurl across the sky where someone
has pinned up a secondhand moon
like a lost object hanging
in the laundromat unclaimed.

With the Name Goes Great Responsibility

i.

Be impatient with the device.
That's what I tell the young people.

The sources are hidden deep within
beyond the fingers of appetite
wrapped in a terrifying envelope
invisibly encoded.

Silence is not just the motto here,
it's the theme of our praise.
Clenched lips betoken honour
remote from the boundaries of response
beneath the awareness of sound
below the enemy's radar.

ii.

The name is ritual and if
it involves some destruction
they're sorry it cannot be helped.

The name is synonymous
with the death of landscape.
There's not even industry with
which to commune, only danger
minus relief or exhilaration.

When you speak the name
you spit poison in highly concentrated form.
With the name goes great responsibility
and even greater fear.
It's tainted don't mouth it

or answer to it.
You're guilty of uttering
when you say it out loud,
manslaughter when you linger
over the intent.

Opportunities for Redemption

Deliverance in the nick of time
is the highlight of my day,
the part I look forward to
and reflect on at night
during someone else's watch;
I imagine you are the same.

The rites of degustation
still mark the few of us who
were not ruined outright.
We are persons set apart: strangers
often remark that there's
something about the eyes,
they're not sure what exactly.

So we are brought to this place
by a twist of character
with its own vocabulary of
evasion and desire.
At this elevation we can hold
out almost indefinitely.

We monitor the ones down below,
tunnel out of view of those up above.
You think it's perfect, but do
not be misled.
Escape has not been brought to an end
but made permanent instead.
Flight is frozen.
There are no longer destinations
if there ever were.

Chinese Anthology *(excerpts)*

i.

In the mountains this time of year
there are tracks on the frozen lake-beds
to prove with what urgency
and how little purpose
unselfconscious animals have wandered.
The truest line between two points
is often unpredictable,
the journeys themselves inevitable
even when least necessary.

ii.

Wherever I go I end up on this
beach in the fog or drizzle
staring out at these tankers and freighters.
The same ones for months on end but
each night I return to find them
in some new arrangement
outlined with droopy strands of light
& I think how the dark water must
soothe their rusty old bellies.

iii.

One day we will not have to write in code.
One day the machinery of what we forget and what
    we remember will no longer be so crucial.
One day we can stop killing time in the desert.
One day there will be room in the alcove.
One day it won't be such hard work to keep it simple.
One day chaos may not necessarily be a virtue.
One day she will be my rod and my staff.
One day there will be no more blood on the snow.

One day there will be no shock on the other side of the door.
One day all will admire the lightness of her touch
    and see that I was right.
One day you will not have to cross the borders to prove
    that they are real.
One day there will be no more conspiracy.
One day we will reach the statute of limitations.
Day of manumission, joyous time.

Mother Goddess

Just as the goddess rises dripping
from the lake like a woman on
an escalator whose topmost
step knows a moment of glory
on its way to
being reborn

so does the surf keep
slapping the beach like a
punctured tyre going round and round.

Art Criticism

Je suis ici pour faire des achats de dynamite.
—Blaise Cendrars

There are no guarantees
that anything will last
especially when you use
these inferior materials.

Thick chemical gesso
slides onto recycled canvas
one coat horizontal
the next vertical;
as soon as one dries,
another arrives to
contradict it.

I can't stand the silence.
My ears chafe waiting
for the tune of a catchy explosion.
I am the neighbourhood dynamiter
who never knows when opportunity
might strike. One must always
be alert and heavily armed
against success and its enemies.

This is how I am.
I have no patience
with craft for its own sake
not like the old
Chinese man standing
in his garden every morning
applying more red lacquer
to his coffin.

When the surface is hard
and shiny like a beetle
he will be venerated as only
the ancient dead can be.

I will be scattered over a wide area.
Parts of me may never be found.

Juice

God grant us juice and the will to share it;
the knowledge to distinguish the lords from the tyrants;
the courage to say what we have to say and get off the stage
(wisdom of any kind accepted most gratefully);
the resolve not to curse when miracles don't happen
(files were kept open ten full years — that's long enough);
the strength to know we don't need respectability or even desire it;
the sense to settle for constant reinvention in the absence of life
   everlasting;
the faith to resort to wild prayers at the last possible moment.

I did not want to show you what I have become
I did not want to shock you with how I have decayed
I did not want to be condemned to this.
Whosoever believeth in me is one sorry animal indeed
that belongs to the wrong club and hath no future
but whosoever believeth in you shall require no further insurance:
one policy covers all catastrophes, the reservoir of our commonality.

I flatter myself that I now believe I know what I was intended to learn.
Is this not a blessed state in which to find oneself when so many others
are cut off prematurely or without understanding the task at all?
I am ready for my next assignment if there is one.
In either case, I sit here watching an old woman in a straw hat
who leads her buffalo home from the fields.

Indonesia

Ice Ages

The grievances stopped
bleeding long ago,
have healed themselves invisibly,
but the grief lingers on
like scars on the lungs
that can't be seen on X-rays.

If I listen closely I can
hear the terrible gouging rumbles
of the glacier bearing down.

Long in the future
as the earth recounts the
story of the pain
people will still marvel
at the deep scores in the rock.

Old Chinese Poem

The only road there is likewise the only road back.
New fighting has broken out along the frontier
(new fighting has forever broken out along the frontier).
Mist in the jagged mountain passes fogs men's vision
blurs politics and the difference between pilgrims and bandits.
A figure stands up in the stirrups, surveying the landscape.
The crooked line of refugees is strung out for many *li*
proceeding slowly and with difficulty, like a trickle of water
running uphill.

Bush Architecture

I have come here to avoid the twitter of fax machines heralding spring
with all its factually transmitted diseases.

I have crossed contaminated ground for a privacy of outlook
and the promise of three weeks' hard labour with all the wrong tools.

No ambulance screams where wolves used to be, no stinging tear gas
of nostalgia, but lakes the colour of mercury and news of long ago.

I sweat with spade and pick, groan and pant with axe and maul
far from the theatre of our misunderstanding with its painted wounds
and plans deranged by time.

To write even this much is to risk being called as a material witness,
possibly an accessory during and after the fact,
or else to hide myself in other people's unsanctioned lives like the snake
in the chifforobe that bites the lady dressing for the ball.

The cabin has no table and only one chair (held together by a wire
    coat-hanger).
Every morning I haul my water and the wood to heat it with.
The stove is as tight as a good alibi.
Back there, beyond the mountains, the perfection of means is the
    confusion of ends.

I obey only the grammar of weather. One day all language will revert
to truth. No singulars no plurals, no active and no passive verbs.
No case no mood no person no tense. Every word will be usable as any
part of speech. Poetry will have returned to pictures.

0930

She went too near the border at 0930. Thereafter no therapy
was strong enough to call her back.
We mourn that we don't know who our ancestors were.
This is how we occupy ourselves until the gongs sound and the dead
stroll again and exiles go home.
We wait and feel the magnetism that pulls all rivers
towards the sea. All of them but this one, like a trace of blood
trickling from the corner of the mouth, drying in the sun,
evidence decaying into archives, a splinter of
someone else's recollection, beyond the reach of reconstituted feeling.

The first injection is only a warning, the second
is where their intentions repose.
Suddenly you don't hear the birds anymore.
Then you see the bridge lights,
warnings not to be ignored.
The next morning, a perfect outburst like tropical rain.
The doctor has died again but the patient lives.
An all-inclusive darkness has accumulated.
Now night is rescinded, dawn remodelled, doom rescheduled.
The possibilities are re-examined in light of startling new photos.

Letter Two *(excerpt)*

In times gone by, I preferred a still earlier period.
The older people seemed more alive to me, and I would try to
visualise them as the wild-fox spirits they had been.
They would recall when cities were the normal means of being.
The stories they could tell of Winnipeg in its glory!
Going there now is like visiting a ruin no one reveres.
In those days, people came and went on streetcars
up and down Portage Avenue.
If you see such a streetcar today, run, or stand perfectly still;
it may not be stopping for you this time.

I would go to thrift shops searching for the rejected books,
the most obsolete clothes, thoroughly discarded decorative objects.
I made a little museum on the walls of my bedroom. There were old
newspapers, photographs on stiff card of unidentified persons
thrown out when other persons died, Second World War ration
tokens, advertisements which had lost all their context, leaving
only their design, which I cherished. Now when I sink back
into the past, it is to this world, not the intervening one
I've seen grow old around me (and me with it).

History was a mistake.
I mistook it for something that was still there. At the present rate
the world gives birth to a new Mexico City each year (with Mexico
itself swelling all the time). Half the world's people
live in cities but hate one another. Epidemics do their best
to round off the total to the nearest billion.
Can history have any meaning in a moment this vast?
That's the question no one asks directly. It doesn't come up
in interviews or dinner party conversation. We all fear
that yesterday has no precedent worth applying.
There I've said it and I'm glad.

Singer, An Elegy *(excerpts)*

i.

He stopped when the music stopped
stopped when the night stopped.

Memory is the last surviving document.
Hearsay evidence is all I hear said

inside the night silence when
important stuff rises to the surface at last.

Hard to judge what number he'd been given
as all those files have disappeared.

Hard to know where he was slotted in the world
he loved, sensing how the past's decay

makes the present possible — "a wide open town"
he could get in step with.

The moderns fought for fun with
blood the prize.

The map was a tall isosceles triangle.
He felt at home between its wide shoulders

in old frame houses and in factories and plants
with their names in black block letters

on white rectangles painted on the dirty bricks:
MILLING & MACHINE — SOUTH END WORKS.

Miles were longer then and cities in motion
and that which he knew, he knew.

I suppose he was a bit like Thoreau who
"travelled widely in Concord"

but his style was more like Whitman, a machine man
who liked to get his hands dirty learning

how things worked. He cleaned
and embellished in a single motion,

hiding some facts, discovering others.
"Nobody's any the wiser."

I can't know if he was depressed
because he had just one mood (happy enough)

and only one mode (getting along fine
in the circumstances).

He perfected the etiquette
of letting others think he wasn't all

that complex. With such filters he couldn't
be buffaloed.

Many were fooled but others weren't,
detecting a style of being in the world

like the trace of some outgrown accent
hinting at higher expectations

abandoned overthrown ignored renounced.
Nouns say no more than verbs:

self-destruction exile bad luck asceticism
hard-times gumption peace and quiet

get-up-and-go.
He was of a different syntactical type

dreaming adjectives but living adverbs
so that most of what I know of him

I've learned from myself by myself.
The mirror compares unfavourably

with seventy-year-old snapshots
and my ignorance is no less anguished.

I think of him photographing a buddy of his
then turning the camera on himself.

A click rings out.
An image falls to the ground.

ii.

He was patient with the present
no doubt too patient,

tolerant of the future
perhaps foolishly.

He kept the important
parts of the past to himself

where I couldn't find them
without knowing there were questions to ask

much less knowing the right ones.
For him, I believe, it all came down

to not having anyone to confide in,
only a superficial beer-joint buddy

and a kid too young to understand what
was going on.

But I sensed there were places
to know where even someone snooping

on his own dreams must make a selection
from all the disasters being offered.

If his life was like mine and other people's,
choices rushed up and completely filled

his field of vision and he reacted,
hoping for the best. Make the wrong

decision and choice recedes to a dot
that disappears. When nightmare

takes over the carnival midway,
the calliope plays screams.

iii.

To be eighteen then was to feel
cheated and be scared. That's how I imagine it

recalling that old mnemonic device —
unemployment hits 33 per cent in 1933.

But this is an aid to remembering what he
wished to forget but couldn't.

What little tricks do we use with ourselves
to disregard or ignore outright?

In this area he was blessed with riches
on whose interest I scrape by.

I also grieve because grief has defined
me this way with whatever strength I have.

I've remained an outsider among the dead
since we traded places — he leaving, I staying behind,

there's such a chilling neatness to
continuity of this sort.

Another grief requires a degree
of concentration I've never shown.

It's a state of awareness I've kept myself from
by doing whatever I've done. Now that I've determined

I failed, it flows back over me like a welcoming tide.
Who knew it could be this warm?

I feel completed by not being whole
and pray that for you the reverse is true.

This is as much philosophy as I know at present.
Nothing so far has compensated. Sometimes I distract

myself for a moment, nothing more.
Am I worthy of what I feel?

The arithmetic of it is facile, but one
can't say glibly that the ground turned to quicksand

when he hit thirty and the soldiers came home.
What I hear are missteps well on their way to

becoming a run, a rout in fact,
in a lethal acceleration that could neither

be predicted nor stopped once underway
but withstood with a dignity that didn't seem

dignified to others more fortunate,
or less. It took courage

to look for past warmth when this morning was
worn and brown, to bum for work with a soft voice

and go on the road at two cents a mile
to the cities that drained the countryside

but also to towns no railway sought as you did
those restaurants Recommended by Duncan Hines

and other comforts along the highways
with motor courts spurned for a proper hotel.

Of course speed is courage especially to the young
but so is distance covered. Freedom is courage

and so is self-confinement.
Hotels can be courage

if you know how to use them.
They're part of a strategy.

iv.

At some stage death ceases to seem
such a distant epidemic

and so he died and in time
the city followed, money

getting scarce and crowds grown thin,
upper storeys abandoned first

(red Xs in never-washed windows
signifying vacancies),

then the rot crept lower until finally
the ground floor too is boarded up and painted over

as though the owners could fool
us into believing they'd make a

fresh start when things got better.
Once he earned a living being young.

He never had the chance to earn a living being old.
In between, he made his own hand tools

which was cheaper than buying.
He had to be satisfied with the craft

when he used them to build machinery
that helped make more machinery.

The literal was also metaphor.
"He's a real piece of machinery, that one is!"

A character, a card. The heart is
an engine of sorts. "Be careful

when you give it the gun. You'll
flood it."

He got a friend to weld
a homemade hasp on the heavy tool chest

though it never knew a lock.
Snub-nose pliers and needle-nose pliers,

vice-grips, drills and bits,
a ball-peen hammer, scribers and punches,

files. A micrometer.
A small pair of bow-handled wire strippers

with a quarter-inch wrench on the end of one arm.
He must have dreamed up that one

for a particular job and thought it too good to throw out.
He stencilled his initials on the head

of an eight-pound sledge and the handle
of a carpenter's saw. Other stuff.

Much other stuff.
There was a good quality whetstone its original

cardboard box now frayed and below that folded clippings
from a "men's magazine." Something about the Quarter

in New Orleans and "the old Gaslight Club in Chicago"
where the women wore shoes net stockings and

nothing else. Finding these
a boy grew excited then sad

about rivers coming to an end in denial and frustration.
There were six, eight integrated mills making

steel from scratch not from other people's scrap.
At night the sky was orange in Aetnaville

so named by someone with a classical education
who also owned the whorehouses.

They were profitable in themselves and a necessary cost
of doing business to keep the hunkies happy

micks spics greaseballs they'd turn commie
in a minute unless kept busy fighting one another.

In wartime the plants went twenty-four hours:
three shifts. Men learned who was hiring the same way

packs of dogs learn where food is.
Now the centre was cooling and the edges

where he lived breaking away.
He'd rather be down in New Orleans

with chicory in the coffee, oysters for breakfast
if you wanted then apple pandowdy for dessert,

a band always playing just out of hearing and people
who know what decay is for, not up north

making his own tools like a slave
turned blacksmith shackling himself.

Baskets full of tools.
He needed a long life to live off such metal fruit.

     v.

When one of the fluorescent lights
grew old it made a sound like insects

buzzing then flickered then died.
The one on the left gave out often,

a short most likely congenital, so
he shaved with half his face in shadow,

the nicks on the skin making signs that said
one part of his body was already condemned

and the other condemned to follow.
He knew where the bootleggers went

for brewer's yeast in bricks
and he'd dissolve some in boiling water

to treat the infection in his poor inflamed lung
on the left side where the heart is.

vi.

She was a Forties person whom the war might rescue

though that's all she grasped of it.
(She once told me Hitler was a communist and

that's as much as she needed to know.)
He while younger was a Thirties type,

a New Dealer, a product more of ruin than of decay
who found his family on the other side of the crevasse

once Earth broke apart right
where they were standing.

Everything conspired to wreck her mind
already weak. Alcohol begging the rage,

even poor eyesight urging paranoia;
they were depressed in incompatible ways.

She did not understand what was taking place
and turned violent like an animal

already rabid. He sensed the presence of fate.
Luck created the problem, now let luck fix it,

allow events to resolve themselves,
inertia to run its course

without prejudice or external pressures.
I was caught in a marriage once, I understand

better now.
I remember him taking a long thin pole

to measure the level in the cisterns.
I remember how he ordered a ton of coal

delivered down the chute each autumn with a volcanic roar
and a large bloom of fine black powder.

Eventually the noise evaporated and the particles
in the air reunited with their source.

I see him stoking the furnace at five a.m.
sending the heat of Hell up through ducts to the hell above,

then using the handle of the shovel to slam
the cast-iron door in the face of circumstance.

vii.

Always more people to be mourned
always new people to grieve for them

but only so much feeling.
In charnel house days, the bones of

the freshly dead went in,
those of the others came out –

the ones of those no longer recalled even distantly.
In the end, it all has to do with memory

going forward not looking down
and then not glancing back.

But there's a great deal of this sorrow going round;
some of us catch it like the flu.

The elegy now like the eulogy then
does nothing for its subject

perhaps nothing for the listener either.
It once may have helped the devout

attenuate themselves to imagine they
saw the scene as the

dead themselves might do,
looking down knowingly, powerless, keeping

the link open. For a while it may help
blow air on recollection, making it lurch

in the fire it then becomes a part of,
warning of pain in some,

anaesthetising others: a matter of
temperament mostly

permitting us to evade
the memory but remember the elegist.

Tennyson tells us almost nothing about Hallam
whose existence we wouldn't know of otherwise

but something more of the writer himself
and so too here, I suppose:

a textbook example of
someone still alive with desire

starting to close
and no one to delegate the remembrance to

in an ever more accepting agony
for another born almost a century ago

and dead now nearly half as long:
the methodical pain of accident

extended mathematically forever
even after the last person who remembers

forgets and is himself or herself forgotten.
Elegies are funerals we conduct on paper to

make ourselves feel
better which, when temporary, survivors are welcome to

overhear, a totally unsatisfying legacy
on the deaths that are suicides of a sort

and the others that are merely executions.
A prayer to the river gods might commence:

Please I can't die yet, there's
so much healing still to do.

That would be mine. Would it also
be his? I don't know how

we struggle on as we do . . .

viii.

At the centre of the city is the cemetery where the dead
assemble to mock us with their strength and neatly

crosshatched streets and alleys, but there's no
direct route from the polished granite neighbourhood ("ritzy")

to the poor slate ones the wind plunders of statistics.
The graveyard city is a scandalous attack on what we know

passing itself off as satire.
My best excuse for why I didn't write this long ago

is that I've spent all these years in transit
to get past the shock I can't forget and

outstay this most superficial grief;
what I can't overcome is the loss I feel even more sharply

as he recedes and I follow, the way generations are intended to do
by the process that deposits us back at the basics

against our will. No wonder we're in a turmoil all the time.
Hard as I tried to save it, I have forgotten the voice,

remembering merely its irony and gentleness,
but not the rest, for I seem to inhabit his appearance

like a suit of someone else's clothes
and this pleases me and terrifies in equal measure

often and especially right before sunrise.
The truth may be that the body is designed for fifty years'

hard use with no intermission. If so, he beat the odds
by a margin heartbreakingly spare to perform a death

that made so little difference to the map
that the characters still standing at the bar down the street

couldn't remember him or recognise the name
a short twenty years later when I sneaked in

for a fast bit of homage and a bitter glass of beer:
a life, that is, more interim than most or many or some,

hobbled by left-side vulnerability and conditions ambient
in the world, but not failed by any means, I've learned,

for he was wiser, kinder, still more tolerant, more
tranquil with the momentum that carries us along

more of everything at the close than at the start,
though events and sensations were rushed

towards the end, as the day reached the point it reaches
and he thanked those who protected him until he died

and life for me began in earnest;
he passed it to me like a baton in a relay race

and it cripples me to realise how little I've done.
I sweat tears to think about it and him; the two are no longer distinct.

I've read the literature of this wretched devastation
but feel nothing I haven't already said myself

expressed in my own arid idioticon
waiting for streetcars that don't exist.

First Signs of Wartime Spring

Eleven ships in English Bay this morning
impatient for their turn at the gantries
ten or more every day so far this month
business in China must be good
cherry blossoms underfoot like confetti
once the echoes evaporate
I leave my footprints until the next breeze.

The Americans have a new war
that's how we know the generations have changed
but we're not headlines we don't need verbs
to validate ourselves.
To the east, the shoulder of the sky is hunched
in back of the sun, still arguing for acceptance
begging us to go there.
The strategy is to let the future emerge
a little at a time that we might grow accustomed
and not protest or go mad.
The window opens so briefly that we cannot
throw out the words.
This will have to do for now.

Mountains to the north zoom in
on people currently between destinations
it's time to harvest the lessons
tomorrow is deep yesterday shallow
sometimes the other way round.
Be like the cave-dwelling hermit
who learns from the mute and mocks
the big yellow bruise.
Slideshow over, the screen goes white
we revert to ritual avoidance of rituals
as practised by lordly bureaucrats who seldom
deviate from what they receive.

The meaningless courage of the entourage
fails them as usual.

Dawn dusk inhale exhale
at night when the stars tremble
we will have no comfort to offer
consumed as we are in events we observe
yet refuse to follow.

Old before my time in relation
to the time available
I spend my declining years declining to accept
struggling to continue trusting the voice
that is the public function of the heart.
In the end, succour finds its own level
everyone fingers everybody else
everyone forgives everybody else
we're all subsidiaries of one another
whatever I know I've learned by
eavesdropping.

Vancouver, April 2005

Navigating Chinatown

Kamikaze snows dive to their death once street lamps lure them with fraudulent hopes. Visibility so poor, collars turned up so high, tuques pulled down so low that I barely make out your silhouette tromping along beside me up Spadina to wherever it may lead us. We try not to think about destinations but cannot help ourselves, nostalgic as we are for the time when there was more life left. The grievous cold and injured dark assign us roles. Navigating Chinatown.

Thanks to this process called mortality we retain little of what we were yet remain as much strangers to each other as once we were only to ourselves. Separating etiquette from survival has never been difficult for people like us. To ask someone what name he used in the old country was rude at best and probably dangerous. Questions were the leading cause of death in males sixteen to seventy-five. Our understanding of these courtesies has helped us persist as safely as we have thus far. It has also diminished us to the size we are this evening.

Trying to sort out what things to forget before both of us buckle like two bad knees. We're not here to rush but there's time enough only for candour. Were you ever in the business of getting passports for deserters? No, that was somebody else, I remember now. Spadina isn't Jewish any more. On a distant day it won't be Chinese either. But it will still be Spadina full of people who never knew anyone who remembered somebody who once saw us when we were alive. The land of farflung afterthoughts bids you welcome.

Confusion of Themes Not of Motives

Poems should be wisdom or be love.
Deficient in one I am overstocked in the other
and it must remain my secret that the inventory will be yours
coming to you someday as a puzzling bequest.

The worst sort of ignorance is the kind that bears my name.
It belongs to a prisoner who's locked out and not in
not knowing any possible answers to the questions
I ache to ask, simple questions, the sort
that work their way up through the membranes
in a lifetime of having breakfast.

I was young and narrow without you because I was without you
and the narrowness survived the youth till your appearing cured it.
The middle years were those of anguish and desire.
I thought a great deal about Art Deco as one of the culture's finest
    moments
to which you have remained true so tall sleek streamlined,
elegant in your simplicity of line
acknowledging the machine you rebel against but respecting it
as the hunter does the animal he singles out:
a private matter between creatures just like the subject at hand.
Your palette of earth tones should be viewed in full sunlight.
You are terra cotta with trim of muted silver.
You are my landmark.

Mappamundi*

Autumn has come and leaves blow aloft
like kites torn apart by competing winds.
At this distance you can't hear the clouds
colliding but only the rain being blotted
on the pavement. Twigs snap. Bones snap.
So many dead.

With untidy mystical visions of the strangers
who need their rest, summon all the travellers
passing through. Bring them together,
hear the conversations of watchful couples
not like us but grown old together, replying
to either's silence with silence of the two together.

Cracks in the ceiling plaster are the rivers
of your body. In the patterns of the mutilated lino
I find faces, yours and those of saints and
everybody's favourite sacred parent.
People always mock me for reinventing
myself, as though this were more than
a form of reincarnation in which we can
all believe. New formats, old loves. Ripening.

You had an insurmountable head start
when I first saw you descending
outfitted in accomplishment top to toe.
Who am I to be blessed by if not by
the one with little stomach for such stupidity
as catching both a cold and an overdose?
It is good that you reject me to keep me even

---

* 'A map for contemplation, not for use.'

or so I have believed once or twice.
At this time of year there is heightened
danger of desire.

Postdated

Facing the nightmare
of another winter encampment
starving within sight of the enemy's fires,
late-modern armies often surrendered
in October, the month when death-notices
fill so many columns in the morning papers.

We must not concede just yet
merely from being so worn down
but carefully slowly grow the letters.
However little time remains
still we mustn't hurry: last words
should be words made to last.

'I'm leaving town until this mess
blows over.'

Afterword

Kenneth Rexroth made a statement in an essay of his that I don't seem able to pinpoint right now in any of his numerous books. As it is an observation I've always admired for its wisdom and insight, I will assume the risk of paraphrasing it as accurately as I can. He said that when African-American musicians travelled inexorably and inevitably up the Mississippi Valley from New Orleans to Chicago, they were also moving away from blues and towards jazz—in the same way that the Russian intelligentsia, following the failed revolution of 1905, abandoned naturalism for the occult. In both instances, he went on, the people involved were seeking a language they knew the police couldn't possibly understand.

I once read the exact quotation to George Woodcock, the anti-authoritarian philosopher, critic and sometime poet at his home in Vancouver. He laughed a wonderful laugh that until then I had never heard him emit, because he was hearing the words of someone who had arrived at the same conclusion as himself, but through a different cultural lens. For it was Woodcock who had commented, repeatedly, I believe, that the making and consumption of poetry slows during periods of peace and political freedom but rises significantly during times of war and repression, when free speech and other civil liberties are most in peril. Both figures knew whereof they spoke. Rexroth was an American, born in 1904; Woodcock, a Canadian, born in 1912. They reached literary adulthood during the 1930s. The betrayals of the Spanish Civil War affected them deeply. Both were conscientious objectors during the Second World War and victims of McCarthyism not long afterwards.

Rereading most of my published poetry now, I see the same principle, the same argument, replayed through the filter of a later generation's voice. It seems to me that the desire to create new codes of hearing—as it were, to address the equivalents of the jazzers and occultists while sidestepping the cops—is one of the two strongest elements in my work. At certain periods, it has been the dominant one. The outlook I describe seems especially suited to my long strings of urban haiku, such as those that make up *Rites of Alienation* (1988). Many other instances of this openly intensive manner can be found in *The Dreams of Ancient Peoples* (1991), *Madagascar: Poems & Translations* (1999), and *The Sylvia Hotel Poems* (2010). The last of these shows my other mode as well: what I call writing-to-heal.

In this second manner, I find myself, as many poets do, working through some of the tragedies, entanglements and insoluble misunderstandings that cause so much stress, remorse and grief. In making this selection, A.F. Moritz, I believe, has shown a strong preference for the first kind of voice over this second, or perhaps it's simply the case that the healing poems have a tendency to go on too long. In any event, readers of this sampler will still hear this second poetic get to its feet from time to time and clear its throat. It often speaks in an elegiac accent. Indeed, one of the relevant books in this category actually is an elegy. A few words about how it came to be written might cast light on the strange ways in which such poems are composed, as when a memory, experience or emotional reaction has been under the skin for so long that it must one day get squeezed out onto the page.

I once met a famous novelist and former war correspondent who had walked about for decades with a piece of shrapnel from the Vietnam War still embedded in one leg. It kept showing up on X-rays. Then one evening it simply worked its way through the skin and fell out onto the dance floor as he and his wife were celebrating their wedding anniversary by performing a vigorous tango. My book *Singer, An Elegy* is the poetic equivalent of that occurrence. In 1994, I published a memoir entitled *Travels by Night*. Once it was out, I began to realize that there were many things I still wished to say, and to understand, about my father, who had died young. I recalled a cinematic dream about his life that I had while travelling in western China. I struggled with the poem somewhat discontinuously, for the material was painful to the touch. The completed work finally appeared in 2004, exactly ten years after the memoir that provoked it into being.

I should add that these two contrasting approaches to writing—the political/public and the therapeutic/restorative—have the same prominence in my prose fiction, though in that genre they are more likely to work together as one. *The File on Arthur Moss* is certainly an engagé book. It derives from an impulse similar to that found, for example, in the novels of André Malraux (but of course this is not a qualitative statement). Yet buried in the narrative are certain ghosts I was hoping to exorcise through the act of writing. So too with the quite different books that followed: *Jericho, Tales of Two Cities: A Novella Plus Stories* and *Walt Whitman's Secret*.

Speaking of Whitman, I note in my poetry a weakness for making lists, somewhat similar to Whitman's but of different parentage. Whitman's love of lists seemed to derive from his days in newspaper journalism; they are compilations of facts. Mine, by contrast, have been suggested by the urge to name, and especially to enumerate, found throughout much of Chinese literature and culture. Reading Al Moritz's brief selection of my poetry invisibly italicizes the small number of keywords that have been recurring in my writing for decades. His choices also appear to detect and then emphasize a certain spiritual quality in a way I, or any other less astute editor, probably would not have been able to do. Yet, as the order is roughly (but not rigidly) chronological, one can see the slow cross-fade between the young poet who teased death and the old one who takes it very seriously indeed. At some point in the process, it seems to me, I ceased writing to myself, or speaking to others through a thin veil, and started to address the reader more directly in a different tongue and in a spirit of fellowship, born of the realization that we're all in this joyous mess together.

—*George Fetherling*

Acknowledgements

From *Subroutines* (Toronto: League of Canadian Poets, 1981)
    "Subroutine"
    "Border Catechism"

From *Variorum* (Toronto: Hounslow Press, 1985)
    "Alleycat"
    "Harry's New York Bar in Paris"
    "The Dark Grid"
    "The Six O'Clock News from Buffalo"

From *Moving towards the Vertical Horizon* (Toronto: Subway Books, 1986)
    "Moving towards the Vertical Horizon"

From *The Dreams of Ancient Peoples* (Toronto: ECW Press, 1991)
    "Memorandum for the File"
    "Pre Texts"
    "Radio"

From *Chinese Anthology* (Victoria, BC: Reference West, 1992)
    "Chinese Anthology"

From *Madagascar: Poems & Translations* (Windsor, ON: Black Moss Press, 1999)
    "Juice"
    "Ice Ages"
    "Old Chinese Poem"
    "Bush Architecture"
    "0930"
    "Letter Two"

From *Singer, An Elegy* (Vancouver: Anvil Press, 2004)
    "Singer, An Elegy"

From *Selected Poems* (Vancouver: Subway Books, 2005)
    "Ancient Beliefs"
    "Telegraphic Instructions"
    "Beginning with North"

"The View Keeps Reminding Us of Flags"
"With the Name Goes Great Responsibility"
"Opportunities for Redemption"
"Mother Goddess"
"Art Criticism"

From *The Sylvia Hotel Poems* (Toronto: Quattro Books, 2010)
"First Signs of Wartime Spring"
"Navigating Chinatown"
"Confusion of Themes Not of Motives"
"Mappamundi"
"Postdated"

lps Books in the Laurier Poetry Series
Published by Wilfrid Laurier University Press

Dionne Brand *Fierce Departures: The Poetry of Dionne Brand*, edited by Leslie C. Sanders, with an afterword by Dionne Brand • 2009 • xvi + 44 pp. • ISBN 978-1-55458-038-5

Di Brandt *Speaking of Power: The Poetry of Di Brandt*, edited by Tanis MacDonald, with an afterword by Di Brandt • 2006 • xvi + 56 pp. • ISBN-10: 0-88920-506-X; ISBN-13: 978-0-88920-506-2

Nicole Brossard *Mobility of Light: The Poetry of Nicole Brossard*, edited by Louise H. Forsyth, with an afterword by Nicole Brossard • 2009 • xxvi + 118 pp. • ISBN 978-1-55458-047-7

George Elliott Clarke *Blues and Bliss: The Poetry of George Elliott Clarke*, edited by Jon Paul Fiorentino, with an afterword by George Elliott Clarke • 2008 • xviii + 72 pp. • ISBN 978-1-55458-060-6

Dennis Cooley *By Word of Mouth: The Poetry of Dennis Cooley*, edited by Nicole Markotić, with an afterword by Dennis Cooley • 2007 • xxii + 62 pp. • ISBN-10: 1-55458-007-2; ISBN-13: 978-1-55458-007-1

Lorna Crozier *Before the First Word: The Poetry of Lorna Crozier*, edited by Catherine Hunter, with an afterword by Lorna Crozier • 2005 • xviii + 62 pp. • ISBN-10: 0-88920-489-6; ISBN-13: 978-0-88920-489-8

Christopher Dewdney *Children of the Outer Dark: The Poetry of Christopher Dewdney*, edited by Karl E. Jirgens, with an afterword by Christopher Dewdney • 2007 • xviii + 60 pp. • ISBN-10: 0-88920-515-9; ISBN-13: 978-0-88920-515-4

Don Domanski *Earthly Pages: The Poetry of Don Domanski*, edited by Brian Bartlett, with an afterword by Don Domanski • 2007 • xvi + 62 pp. • ISBN-10: 1-55458-008-0; ISBN-13: 978-1-55458-008-8

Louis Dudek *All These Roads: The Poetry of Louis Dudek*, edited by Karis Shearer, with an afterword by Frank Davey • 2008 • xx+ 70 pp. • ISBN 978-1-55458-039-2

George Fetherling *Plans Deranged by Time: The Poetry of George Fetherling*, edited by A.F. Moritz, with an afterword by George Fetherling • 2012 • xviii + 64 pp. • ISBN 978-1-55458-631-8

M. Travis Lane *The Crisp Day Closing on My Hand: The Poetry of M. Travis Lane*, edited by Jeanette Lynes, with an afterword by M. Travis Lane • 2007 • xvi + 86 pp. • ISBN-10: 1-55458-025-0; ISBN-13: 978-1-55458-025-5

Tim Lilburn *Desire Never Leaves: The Poetry of Tim Lilburn*, edited by Alison Calder, with an afterword by Tim Lilburn • 2007 • xiv + 50 pp. • ISBN-10: 0-88920-514-0; ISBN-13: 978-0-88920-514-7

Eli Mandel *From Room to Room: The Poetry of Eli Mandel*, edited by Peter Webb, with an afterword by Andrew Stubbs • 2011 • xviii + 66 pp. • ISBN 978-1-55458-255-6

Steve McCaffery *Verse and Worse: Selected and New Poems of Steve McCaffery 1989–2009*, edited by Darren Wershler, with an afterword by Steve McCaffery • 2010 • xiv + 76 pp. • ISBN 978-1-55458-188-7

Don McKay *Field Marks: The Poetry of Don McKay*, edited by Méira Cook, with an afterword by Don McKay • 2006 • xxvi + 60 pp. • ISBN-10: 0-88920-494-2; ISBN-13: 978-0-88920-494-2

Al Purdy *The More Easily Kept Illusions: The Poetry of Al Purdy*, edited by Robert Budde, with an afterword by Russell Brown • 2006 • xvi + 80 pp. • ISBN-10: 0-88920-490-X; ISBN-13: 978-0-88920-490-4

F.R. Scott *Leaving the Shade of the Middle Ground: The Poetry of F.R. Scott*, edited by Laura Moss, with an afterword by George Elliott Clarke • 2011 • xxiv + 72 pp. • ISBN 978-1-55458-367-6

Fred Wah *The False Laws of Narrative: The Poetry of Fred Wah*, edited by Louis Cabri, with an afterword by Fred Wah • 2009 • xxiv + 78 pp. • ISBN 978-1-555458-046-0

www.ingramcontent.com/pod-product-compliance
Lightning Source LLC
Chambersburg PA
CBHW060504080526
44584CB00015B/1537